Team Themes

Team Themes

Introduction

I have always been a coach that wanted to inspire my players and coaching staff. Teaching life lessons is the reason I became a coach. Football was simply a tool for me to impact other people.

Because of this, I have always attempted to do themes for our team to get them to think of a larger purpose than just a game. We usually would do an overall theme – for me that has been "Find A Way". We have also done a yearly theme and even weekly themes.

Creating new content of coming up with themes has been difficult at times and can be very tough in the middle of a season. Often, I have relied on quotes and built a theme from these quotes. In this book you will find some of my favorite and powerful quotes.

Feel free to use these as needed. I hope this can create some discussion points for your team and inspiration for you and your staff during the difficult times we all face. My contact information is:

FBCoachSimpson@gmail.com
334-549-9382

# What is in this book?

This book is broken into 2 major parts:

Quotes to motivate the team and coaches
These quotes are meant to inspire you as the coach or your assistants. They are quotes I have gone to for inspiration and motivation each season. They also apply to every member of your team.

Theme quotes
You will find 14 potential themes that I have included with some of my favorite quotes. I hope this may get you started to share themes with your players. It was by far one of the best things I have ever done as a coach.

The goal of this book is to work through with your program and teach more than just a game to your program.

At the end of each section, I have included some basic questions we would talk with our team about. Feel free to use these or add your own as you work to make your program about more than the game.

There is also a QR code at the end of each section that will link to a motivational video over the topic.

Table of Contents

Quotes for the Team

Quotes for the Team

"Football is a great game, but is a terrible god".
-Randy Ragsdale

"In order to win the game, you must first not lose it."
-Chuck Noll

"You don't win with X's and O's. What you win with is people."
-Joe Gibbs

"Coaches have to watch for what they don't want to see and listen to what they don't want to hear."
-John Madden

"Leadership, like coaching, is fighting for the hearts and souls of men and getting them to believe in you."
—Eddie Robinson

Quotes for the Team

"If anything goes bad, I did it. If anything goes semi-good, we did it. If anything goes really good, then you did it. That's all it takes to get people to win football games for you."
-Bear Bryant

"Many people erroneously think they have only one chance to succeed, and if they miss that chance, they are doomed to failure. In fact, most people have several opportunities to succeed."
-Bill Walsh

"If you're just saying, hey, I'm doing this. I'm working to make money. I'm working to increase my status. If that's all there is, I think you will find out that it's meaningless."
-Tony Dungy

"When you win, say nothing, when you lose, say less."
—Paul Brown

Quotes for the Team

"After all the cheers have died down and the stadium is empty, after the headlines have been written, and after you are back in the quiet of your room and the championship ring has been placed on the dresser and after all the pomp and fanfare have faded, the enduring thing that is left is the dedication to doing with our lives the very best we can to make the world a better place in which to live."
-Vince Lombardi

"Never give up on a dream just because of the time it will take to accomplish it. The time will pass anyway."
-Earl Nightingale

"Many of the great achievements of the world were accomplished by tired and discouraged men and women who kept on working."
—Anonymous

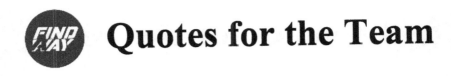

Quotes for the Team

"Things may come to those who wait, but only the things left by those who hustle."
–Abraham Lincoln

"The man who succeeds is a man who has withstood the tests of time, trials, and has made every effort count."
-Hermann J. Steinherr

"When someone tells me 'no,' it doesn't mean I can't do it, it simply means I can't do it with them."
-Karen E. Quinones Miller

"It isn't the mountains ahead to climb that wear you out; it's the pebble in your shoe."
-Muhammad Ali

Quotes for the Team

"Don't wait until everything is just right. It will never be perfect. There will always be challenges, obstacles, and less than perfect conditions. So what? Get started now. With each step you take, you will grow stronger and stronger, more and more skilled, more and more self-confident, and more and more successful."
-Mark Victor Hansen

"You're never too old. One winter I was down in the Phoenix area and this man I met, he and I would meet on the track every Tuesday. I'd be doing my workout, he'd be doing his. He was training for the Boston Marathon and he was 75."
-Shalane Flanagan

"And I understood that in an age where there was so much ego, because of the camera, that it was very important to look for that kind of player ... I began to look for the kind of player that doesn't need his ego fed by stardom, but will do what he's supposed to do because he knows the game and loves the game, and will do the job the right way even if someone else gets the glory."
-Bill Belichick

Team Themes

This section will feature 14 potential themes for your team. Each theme will have 7-10 quotes to use as you relate this topic to life.

Each section will feature a short overview and questions to ask your athletes/coaches as you work to make your program about more than a game.

Topics

Honor
Integrity
Effort
Grit
Sacrifice
Character
Pride
Competitive
Encouraging
Leadership
Commitment
Adversity
Excellence
Winning

Team Themes

Feel free to use this book any way that can help with your team this season. It is also organized to be set up with a game week. For example: If your games are on Friday, it will have daily quotes, questions or examples of that theme each day of the week leading up to game day.

The goal is to use the sport you coach to teach life lessons with your athletes. If this book can start a discussion that will impact one of them, that was the entire goal. Remember that as coaches, we are shaping the next generation.

Honor

Honor

Monday:

Honor is a word that is thrown around often in our society, but never really explained. Having honor is something that is given to certain people, but why? What have they done to deserve honor? How do we increase our ability to have honor?

Working with athletes, often I try express that they cannot control outside factors. How people view or treat them is often beyond our control. But, what we can control is how we act or react to others. If we want to have honor from others, we must first show honor to ourselves.

Live a life that shows we are who we say we are all the time. Through good and bad times our attitude and actions must remain the same. Doing the right thing all the time is very difficult and is why many people cannot achieve this characteristic.

What does the word Honor mean to you?
Does our team show Honor?

Honor

Tuesday:
"Honor isn't about making the right choices. It's about dealing with the consequences."
-Sophocles

"Nobody can acquire honor by doing what is wrong."
-Thomas Jefferson

"He who has lost honor can lose nothing more."
Publilius Syrus

"He who lives without discipline dies without honor."
-Proverb

Which quote stuck out to you the most? Why?

Honor

Wednesday:
"It is little honor to the lion to seize the mouse."
-German Proverb

"Reputation is what other people know about you. Honor is what you know about yourself."
-Lois McMaster Bujold

"The greatest way to live with honor is to be what we pretend to be."
-Socrates

What can you do to become better in this area in your life?

Honor

Thursday Team Review

1) What does the word in this theme mean to you?

2) Which quote stuck out to you the most?

3) **Think of a story in your life or in a friend's life where this theme played out.**

4) Does our team show Honor?

5) What can you do to become better in this area in your life?

Honor

My notes on honor:

Integrity

Integrity

Monday:

Integrity is one of the most difficult ideals to live up to in our daily life. Being the same person through difficult times can be hard. Not lying or cheating when doing so would go unnoticed and get us ahead in life is very tempting. Stabbing someone in the back so that we can take that position has become what much or our culture preaches. Get ahead in life by any means necessary.

Integrity disagrees with this premise 100%. Having integrity means doing the right thing even though it may not be the "best" or "easiest" thing for you personally. Who you are when no one watches is who you really are.

What does the word integrity mean to you? Does our team show integrity?

Integrity

Tuesday:
"Live so that when your children think of fairness, caring, and integrity, they think of you."
-H. Jackson Brown, Jr.

One of the truest tests of integrity is its blunt refusal to be compromised.
-Chinua Achebe

Integrity without knowledge is weak and useless, and knowledge without integrity is dangerous and dreadful.
-Samuel Johnson

"If you value your integrity, then be prepared to take a beating from those who have none."
-Lars Lau Thygesen

Which quote stuck out to you the most? Why?

Integrity

Wednesday:

"In looking for people to hire, look for three qualities: integrity, intelligence and energy. And if they don't have the first, the other two will kill you."
-Warren Buffett

"One of the truest tests of integrity is blunt refusal to be compromised."
-Chinua Achebe

"Integrity — The choice between what's convenient and what's right."
-Tony Dungy

What can you do to become better in this area in your life?

Integrity

Thursday Team Review

1) What does the word integrity mean to you?

2) Which quote stuck out to you the most?

3) **Think of a story in your life or in a friend's life where this theme played out.**

4) Does our team show integrity?

5) What can you do to become better in this area in your life?

Integrity

My notes on integrity:

Effort

Effort

Monday:

Effort is the #1 characteristic I look for when I evaluate athletes. Talent is natural, but effort is something we can control and we decide every day how much we will spend. If you want to prove you care about your team or family, show them by your effort, not your words.

Many of my favorite players to coach were the hardest workers, not the most talented. As a coach, we know our team will be special when our most talented players are also the best with their effort. Those teams will be special.

What does effort mean to you?
Does our team show great effort?

Effort

Tuesday:
"Plough deep while sluggards sleep."
— Benjamin Franklin

"Success in anything will always come down to this: Focus & Effort, and we control both of them."
-Dwayne "The Rock" Johnson

"Effort is only effort when it begins to hurt."
—José Ortega y Gassett

"Mediocre people hate high achievers, and high achievers hate mediocre people."
-Nick Saban

Which quote stuck out to you the most?
Why?

Effort

Wednesday:

"There's not a person on my team in 16 years that has consistently beat me to the ball every play. That ain't got nothing to do with talent, That's just got everything to do with effort, and nothing else."
—Ray Lewis

"Show me a guy who's afraid to look bad, and I'll show you a guy you can beat every time."
—Lou Brock

"Nobody ever drowned in his own sweat."
—Ann Landers

Effort

"If what you did yesterday seems big, you haven't done anything today."
—Lou Holtz

"If a man is a quitter, I'd rather find out in practice than in a game. I ask for all a player has so I'll know later what I can expect."
-Bear Bryant

What can you do to become better in this area in your life?

Effort

Thursday Team Review

1)   What does the word effort mean to you?

2)   Which quote stuck out to you the most?

3)   **Think of a story in your life or in a friend's life where this theme played out.**

4)   Does our team show effort?

5)   What can you do to become better in this area in your life?

Effort

My notes on effort:

Effort

Grit

Grit

Monday:

Grit is the one characteristic that is often the difference between success in life or living the saying, "That guy could have been so good." One of the worst things a coach can say about a player is that they never play up to their potential. Those that are able to play through tough circumstances will ultimately prove to be the more successful people in life.

Possessing "grit" is the one trait I hope to pass on to all athletes I am fortunate to coach. Learning to persevere is a life lesson that we all must face. I have studied many of the most successful coaches and players and each of them are different. Some are outgoing, some are quiet. They come from all different backgrounds as well.

But the one thing every great athlete possesses is GRIT.

What does the word grit mean to you?
Does our team have grit?

Grit

Tuesday:

"Most people give up just when they're about to achieve success. They quit on the one-yard line. They give up at the last minute of the game one foot from a winning touchdown."
–Ross Perot

"The Enemy of the best is the good. If you're always settling with what's good, you'll never be the   best."
-Jerry Rice

"I've missed more than 9,000 shots in my career. I've lost almost 300 games. 26 times, I've been trusted to take the game winning shot and missed. I've failed over and over and over again in my life. And that is why I succeed."
–Michael Jordan

Which quote stuck out to you the most? Why?

Grit

Wednesday:
"The difference between a successful person and others is not a lack of strength, not a lack of knowledge, but rather in a lack of will."
-Vince Lombardi

"You cannot make progress with excuses."
—Cam Newton

"Be not afraid of going slowly; be afraid only of standing still."
-Chinese Proverb

"It ain't about how hard you can hit. It's about how hard you can get hit, and keep moving forward."
—Rocky Balboa

What can you do to become better in this area in your life?

Grit

Thursday Team Review

1) What does the word grit mean to you?

2) Which quote stuck out to you the most?

3) Think of a story in your life or in a friend's life where this theme played out.

4) Does our team show grit?

5) What can you do to become better in this area in your life?

Grit

My notes on grit:

Sacrifice

Sacrifice

Monday:
Being willing to give up personal goals for a greater good is what team sports are all about. Are you willing to allow others to have the spotlight and do the dirty work? Or what about even the work that gets no credit...the scout team.

Teams that are willing to put the team before the individual will always beat those teams that must have the spotlight on specific players. And this lesson carries over in life. Families must sacrifice for each other. Husbands and wives must sacrifice for each other.

The irony is when you are able to put away the selfish thoughts and sacrifice for a greater good. It is very rewarding.

What does the word sacrifice mean to you?
Is our team willing to sacrifice?

Sacrifice

Tuesday:
"The most important decision about your goals is not what you're willing to do to achieve them, but what you are willing to give up."
-Dave Ramsey

"It's not the will to win that matters—everyone has that. It's the will to prepare to win that matters."
—Paul "Bear" Bryant

"If you want something you've never had, you must be willing to do something you've never done."
-Anonymous

"Today I will do what others won't, so tomorrow I will do what others can't."
-Jerry Rice

Which quote stood out to you the most?
Why?

Sacrifice

Wednesday:

"Great achievement is usually born of great sacrifice, and is never the result of selfishness."
-Napoleon Hill

"Success isn't the same as talent. The world is full of incredibly talented people who never succeed at anything."
—Tim Grover

"The difference between a man and a boy, is that a boy only does what he wants to do, but a man does what he has to do."
-Kenny Simpson

What can you do to become better in this area in your life?

Sacrifice

Thursday Team Review

1) What does the word sacrifice mean to you?

2) Which quote stuck out to you the most?

3) **Think of a story in your life or in a friend's life where this theme played out.**

4) Does our team show sacrifice?

5) What can you do to become better in this area in your life?

Sacrifice

My notes on sacrifice:

Character

Character

Monday:

Do you have character, or are you a character is one way to think about this word. Those with character are people that can be trusted. They will be people others are drawn toward. Having character means that a person's word is their bond. They will do what they say 100% of the time even if it will not benefit them.

Athlete's show their character in their sport by showing up on time, giving 100% effort, respecting their team and coaches and more. One of the greatest part of team sports is that it allows young athletes to develop this trait. By doing what is right even when it is difficult, a person grows.

What does the word character mean to you?
Does our team display good character on and off the field?

Character

Tuesday:

"Be more concerned with your character than your reputation. Your character is what you really are, while your reputation is what others think of you."
-John Wooden

"Hard work spotlights the character of people: some turn up their sleeves, some turn up their noses, and some don't turn up at all."
—Sam Ewing

"You learn more about character on the 2-yard line than anywhere else in life."
-Paul Dietzel

Which quote stood out to you the most?
Why?

Character

Wednesday:

"You can't always control circumstances. However, you can always control your attitude, approach, and response. Your options are to complain or to look ahead and figure out how to make the situation better."
-Tony Dungy

"To give anything less than your best is to sacrifice the gift."
-Steve Prefontaine

"The best index to a person's character is how he treats people who can't do him any good, and how he treats people who can't fight back."
-Abigal Van Buren

Character

"Watch your THOUGHTS, they lead to your attitude.

Watch your ATTITUDES, they lead to your words.

Watch your WORDS, they lead to your actions.

Watch your ACTIONS, they lead to your habits.

Watch your HABITS, they lead to your character.

Watch your CHARACTER, it determines your destiny".
-Ralph Waldo Emerson

What do you need to do to work on your character?

Character

Thursday Team Review

1) What does the word character mean to you?

2) Which quote stuck out to you the most?

3) **Think of a story in your life or in a friend's life where this theme played out.**

4) Does our team show character?

5) What can you do to become better in this area in your life?

Character

My notes on character:

Character

Pride

Pride

Monday:
Having pride can mean many different things. But the type of pride this book is referring to is the type of pride that shows respect. Respecting yourself, respecting your team and respecting others. Pride is what we have when we know we have done our very best at whatever we were asked to do.

When I was about 10-years old one of my jobs was to vacuum. My mother would come in and make me do the job over and over until I did it correctly. I just wanted to get it over. That is the difference in a program or a program that has pride. If you have pride in what you are doing, it will be done to the best of your ability every time.

What does the word pride mean to you?
Does our team have pride?

Pride

Tuesday:
"Understand: You should be radiating confidence, not arrogance or disdain." –Robert Greene

"The world will never value you more than you value yourself."
–Bill Masur

"All your life, other people will try to take your accomplishments away from you. Don't you take it away from yourself."
-Michael Crichton

"Your fear of looking stupid is making you look stupid. What other people think of you is none of your business." –Thibaut

Which quote stands out to you the most?
Why?

Pride

Wednesday:

"If you don't have time to do it right, will you have time to do it over?"
—John Wooden

"Be so good they can't ignore you."
—Steve Martin

"No matter how hard it gets, stick your chest up, keep your head high and handle it".
—Unknown

"If you want to be proud of yourself, then do things in which you can take pride".
—Karen Homey

What can you do to become better in this area in your life?

Pride

Thursday Team Review

1) What does the word pride mean to you?

2) Which quote stuck out to you the most?

3) **Think of a story in your life or in a friend's life where this theme played out.**

4) Does our team show pride?

5) What can you do to become better in this area in your life?

Pride

My notes on pride:

Competitive

Competitive

Monday:

The drive to compete is in all of us. This attribute is often what separates winners and losers on the field. While the scoreboard is not the ultimate goal, it is a big one! We should always feel the need to compete and give 100% effort.

Competitors will not always be popular. They will not always win the game, but they do always know they have given everything they have to the cause. True competitors know that often the competition is won before the game is ever played. Preparing to win often separates good from great. Great effort is needed at ALL TIMES.

Learning to compete also involves pushing through. Not quitting when every part of your body and mind want to quit. Fighting even when the game may be for all reasons over. These are the traits you will see when you see a true competitor.

What does the word compete mean to you?
Does our team compete?

Competitive

Tuesday:
"You miss 100 percent of the shots you don't take."
–Wayne Gretzky

"The way to develop self-confidence is to do the thing you fear and get a record of successful experiences behind you."
-William Jennings Bryan

"Success isn't owned, it's leased. And rent is due every day."
-J.J. Watt

"If you see me in a fight with a bear, pray for the bear."
-Kobe Bryant

Which quote stood out to you the most?
Why?

Competitive

Wednesday:
"There are only two options regarding commitment. You're either IN or you're OUT. There is no such thing as life in-between."
—Pat Riley

"When you have a room full of competitors, it's easy to coach. A competitor you prepare; a non-competitor you have to motivate."
-Urban Meyer

"There is winning and there is misery."
-Bill Parcells

What can you do to improve in this area of your life?

Competitive

Thursday Team Review

1) What does the word compete mean to you?

2) Which quote stuck out to you the most?

3) Think of a story in your life or in a friend's life where this theme played out.

4) Does our team compete?

5) What can you do to become better in this area in your life?

Competitive

My notes on competing:

Encouraging

Encouraging

Monday:

Every team needs at least one great encourager. In the best teams it becomes a part of the culture. To be a true encourager requires selflessness. Focusing on others and pushing them to succeed often means we must not be only looking at our own goals.

Part of encouraging is also to tell people what they may not want to hear, but let them know you are there to support them as they try again. On all teams there will come a time when everything seems to go wrong. This is the moment when a true encourager steps up. Motivating others to strive for the common goal is needed in all walks of life, and that applies to all sports as well.

What does encouragement mean to you?
Does our team do a good job encouraging each other?

Encouraging

Tuesday:
"Successful people have fear, successful people have doubts, and successful people have worries. They just don't let these feelings stop them."
- T. Harv Eker

"Make sure your worst enemy doesn't live between your own two ears."
— Laird Hamilton

"Teammates are there for each other even after the noise of the crowd is gone."
-Jim Brown

"A trophy carries dust. Memories last forever."
—Mary Lou Retton

"A word of encouragement after a defeat is worth more than an hour of praise after a success."
-Unknown

Encouraging

"One of the most important things you can do on this earth is to let people know they are not alone."
-Shannon L. Alder

Sometimes one person on your team may not be as strong as another. Strengths usually differ."
- Jake Byrne

"A   rising   tide   lifts   all   boats."
-JFK

Which quote stood out to you the most? Why?

Encouraging

Wednesday:

"When you encourage others, you boost their self-esteem, enhance their self-confidence, make them work harder, lift their spirits and make them successful in their endeavors. Encouragement goes straight to the heart and is always available. Be an encourager. Always."
-Roy Bennett

"There's a misconception about teamwork. Teamwork is the ability to have different thoughts about things; it's the ability to argue and stand up and say loud and strong what you feel. But in the end, it's also the ability to adjust to what is the best for the team."
-Tom Landry

How can you get better at encouraging others?

Encouraging

Thursday Team Review

1) What does the word encouragement mean to you?

2) Which quote stuck out to you the most?

3) **Think of a story in your life or in a friend's life where this theme played out.**

4) Does our team encourage?

5) What can you do to become better in this area in your life?

Encouraging

My notes on encouraging:

 # Encouraging

Leadership

Leadership

Monday:
Being a leader can be a lonely position. It is tough to be willing to put yourself out there for others to ridicule or tear down. However, we need more leaders in our world today. Those willing to help their peers and guide them in the correct path.

Leading can take many forms. Some do it with words and are gifted with speaking the right thing to people or encouraging. Some are quiet and let their actions speak. Leading is not always about being the best or having a specific skill, but it is about caring for those around you and lifting them up.

The hardest part of being a true leader is calling out wrong. This is very difficult as a teenager. If you want the role of a leader you must be willing to stand for what is right and at times against those wanting to do wrong.

What does leadership mean to you?
Does our team have good leadership?

Leadership

Tuesday:

"You can accomplish anything in life provided you don't mind who gets the credit."
- President Harry S. Truman

"You fail all of the time. But you aren't a failure until you start blaming someone else."
-Bum Phillips

"Leadership is the capacity to translate vision into reality".
-Warren Bennis

"If you wait for others to initiate change, you automatically become a follower."
-Peyton Manning

Leadership

"Losers assemble in small groups and complain. Winners assemble as a team and find ways to win."
-Bill Parcells

"A good leader gets people to follow him because they want to, not because he makes them."
-Tony Dungy

"The most important measure of how good a game I played was how much better I'd made my teammates play" – Bill Russell

Which quote stood out to you the most? Why?

Leadership

Wednesday:
"There's a misconception about teamwork. Teamwork is the ability to have different thoughts about things; it's the ability to argue and stand up and say loud and strong what you feel. But in the end, it's also the ability to adjust to what is the best for the team."
-Tom Landry

"Leadership is diving for a loose ball. It's about being able to take it as well as dish it out. That's the only way your going to get respect from other players."
–Larry Bird

What can you do to become a better leader?

Leadership

Thursday Team Review

1) What does the word leadership mean to you?

2) Which quote stuck out to you the most?

3) **Think of a story in your life or in a friend's life where this theme played out.**

4) Does our team have great leaders?

5) What can you do to become better in this area in your life?

Leadership

My notes on leadership:

Leadership

Commitment

Commitment

Monday:

Commitment is not as important in our world today as it used to be. Being willing to stand by our word is difficult and now easy to break. Look at the transfer list for colleges or coaches leaving jobs left and right. It is hard to practice commitment in our world because often it means doing something that is not always easy.

This lesson must be learned or our families will continue to suffer from it. Look at all the fathers that walked out on their commitment today. More than likely half on this team know what that feels like. This lesson is one of the hardest to learn, because we never truly know if we are committed until something difficult arises.

What does the word commitment mean to you? Does our team show commitment to each other?

Commitment

Tuesday:
"Once you learn to quit, it becomes a habit."
-Vince Lombardi

"You have a choice to make when you're not playing. Either you're invested and a great teammate, or you're not."
—Brad Stevens

"Courage is not having the strength to go on; it is going on when you don't have the strength."
-Teddy Roosevelt

"A person really doesn't become whole, until he becomes a part of something that's bigger than himself."
—Jim Valvano

Commitment

"Great players and great teams want to be driven. They want to be pushed to the edge. They don't want to be cheated. Ordinary players and average teams want it to be easy."
—Pat Riley

Which quote stood out to you the most?
Why?

Commitment

Wednesday:

"There's a difference between interest and commitment. When you are interested in something, you do it only when circumstance permit. When you are committed to something, you accept no excuses, only results."
—Art Turock

"Most people fail, not because of lack of desire, but because of lack of commitment."
—Vince Lombardi

What can you do to improve commitment to people that matter?

Commitment

Thursday Team Review

1) What does the word commitment mean to you?

2) Which quote stuck out to you the most?

3) **Think of a story in your life or in a friend's life where this theme played out.**

4) Does our team show commitment?

5) What can you do to become better in this area in your life?

Commitment

My notes on commitment:

Commitment

Adversity

Adversity

Monday:

No one wants adversity to strike. Usually, it hits at the worst time and is not something we are looking for. The question becomes, "How will you handle it when adversity hits you?"

The only way to be ready for adversity is to have a strong conviction in what you are doing, to have encouragers near that will help, and to be willing to stand alone if you must. Each team will go through adversity during the season. Even champions must go through times that are tough. The great teams will rise up, and the average teams will crumble. Make your decision now which you will do.

The real measure of a person is not in times of ease, but in times of adversity. What you have been building inside will come out at that time. Be sure to be preparing for it.

What does overcoming adversity mean to you? Does our team handle adversity well?

Adversity

Tuesday:
"Men are made stronger on realization that the helping hand they need is at the end of their own arm."
— Sidney J. Phillips

"You can learn a line from a win and a book from a defeat."
-Paul Brown

"The person who says it cannot be done should not interrupt the person doing it."
-Chinese Proverb

"Tough times go away, tough people do not."
-Walter Payton

"Never throughout history has a man who lived a life of ease left a name worth remembering."
-Teddy Roosevelt

Which quote stood out the most to you?
Why?

Adversity

Wednesday:

"It is not the critic who counts; not the man who points out how the strong man stumbles, or where the doer of deeds could have done them better. The credit belongs to the man who is actually in the arena, whose face is marred by dust and sweat and blood; who strives valiantly; who errs, who comes short again and again, because there is no effort without error and shortcoming; but who does actually strive to do the deeds; who knows great enthusiasms, the great devotions; who spends himself in a worthy cause; who at the best knows in the end the triumph of high achievement, and who at the worst, if he fails, at least fails while daring greatly, so that his place shall never be with those cold and timid souls who neither know victory nor defeat."
-Teddy Roosevelt

What can you do to improve in how you deal with adversity?

Adversity

Thursday Team Review

1) What does the word adversity mean to you?

2) Which quote stuck out to you the most?

3) **Think of a story in your life or in a friend's life where this theme played out.**

4) Does our team handle adversity?

5) What can you do to become better in this area in your life?

Adversity

My notes on adversity:

Excellence

Excellence

Monday:

Excellence is a very overused word. To become excellent in an area often takes years of practice. While we will never achieve perfection, we can work to achieve excellence. The ability to become a truly elite program is when every part of the program is done right. Many programs are great in areas, but to obtain excellence requires each part.

It is hard to go from bad to good. It is tough to go from good to great. But, it is very difficult to go from great to excellent. Those programs will perform year-in and year-out at a high level. It does not happen overnight. However, it does happen because of several small decisions made each day. When those become the right decision all the time, a program can be considered excellent.

What does excellence mean to you?
Is our team striving for excellence?

Excellence

Tuesday:
"Maturity begins to grow when you can sense your concern for others out-weighing your concern for yourself."
–Phil Jackson

"We are what we repeatedly do. Excellence, therefore is not an act, but a habit."
-Aristotle

"Excellence is not a gift, but a skill that takes practice. We do not act "rightly" because we are "excellent," in fact we achieve "excellence" by acting "rightly."
-Plato

Which quote stood out the most to you?
Why?

Excellence

Wednesday:
"Excellence is the gradual result of always striving to do better."
-Pat Riley

"Every job is a self-portrait of the person who did it. Autograph your work with excellence."
-Jessica Guidobono

"Excellence is to do a common thing in an uncommon way."
-Booker T. Washington

"Excellence is not an exception; it is a prevailing attitude."
-Colin Powell

What can you do to improve yourself as you work towards being excellent?

Excellence

Thursday Team Review

1) What does the word excellence mean to you?

2) Which quote stuck out to you the most?

3) Think of a story in your life or in a friend's life where this theme played out.

4) Does our team shoot for excellence?

5) What can you do to become better in this area in your life?

Excellence

My notes on excellence:

Winning

Winning

Monday:

Herm Edwards said it best when he said, "You play to win the game". The goal of athletics is not just about winning the games, but it is about becoming a winner in all areas of life. We want to win ball games, but more importantly we want to understand the skills and sacrifices needed to win. Take those skills and learn to apply them to all areas in our life.

You can become a winner without being perfect. No one is perfect, but all of us can learn to become winners.

What does the word winning mean to you?
Does our team do everything it takes to win?

Winning

Tuesday:

"Every quarterback can throw a ball; every running back can run; every receiver is fast; but that mental toughness that you talk about translates into competitiveness."
-Tom Brady

"One player's selfish attitude can poison a locker room and make it hard, if not impossible, to establish teamwork."
—Dean Smith

"Teams that play together beat those teams with superior players who play more as individuals."
—Dr. Jack Ramsay

"Do you want to choose winning over standing out? It's a choice every player on every championship team has to do."
—Doc Rivers

Winning

"The difference in winning and losing is often...not quitting."
—Walt Disney

"Winners focus on winning, losers focus on winners."
-Unknown

"Winners develop a habit of what losers don't want to do."
-Unknown

Which quote stood out to you the most? Why?

Winning

Wednesday:
"If you are not willing to learn, no one can help you. If you are determined to learn, no one can stop you."
–Zig Ziglar

"Losers make promises they often break. Winners make commitments they always keep."
–Denis Waitley

"Winners compare their achievements with their goals, while losers compare their achievements to others."
–Nido Qubein

What can you do to improve your chance of being a winner?

Winning

Thursday Team Review

1) What does the word winning mean to you?

2) Which quote stuck out to you the most?

3) **Think of a story in your life or in a friend's life where this theme played out.**

4) Does our team strive to win?

5) What can you do to become better in this area in your life?

Winning

My notes on winning:

Winning

Conclusion

Conclusion

It is my hope that as coaches we are passing on more than just skills and wins on a scoreboard. Hopefully, this guide will be able to serve as a springboard for great conversations with your program. Remember that we only have a short time with our team, but we can make a difference that will last a lifetime.

Work to teach life skills and use the sport you coach as a guide to teach those.

If you have anything I can help with please feel free to reach out:

FBCoachSimpson@gmail.com
334-549-9382
@FBCoachSimpson

About the Author

About the Author

Coach Simpson has served at three schools as the Head Football Coach: Searcy High School, a 6A school in Arkansas in 2020. Before Searcy, he was the Head Football Coach at Southside Charter. Taking over a program that had won eight games in five seasons and had been on a 20+ game losing streak, Simpson led Southside to the playoffs for four-consecutive seasons and won two conference titles in the past three seasons. For his efforts, he was named 4A-2 Conference Coach of the Year (2017), named as a finalist for Hooten's Coach of the Year (2017) and has been the All-Star Nominee for the 4A-2 (2016 and 2019). He was also selected to coach in the 1st FCA Texas-Arkansas All-Star Showdown (2021). Simpson's teams have qualified for the playoffs the past 5 consecutive seasons.

About the Author

Coach Simpson wrote his first book in 2019. He has since released 8 other books. *Find A Way: What I Wish I'd Known When I Became A Head Football Coach,* has been a three-time best seller on Amazon in several categories.

His offense has now run across the globe in not only the United States, but also in South America, Africa, Japan, Europe and Australia. He has helped to install the Gun-T system in many schools over the past 2-years.

Simpson has also raised over $1.5 million for Southside and has overseen several major facility projects including: New Field Turf, Expansion to Fieldhouse, Expansion to the school's home bleachers, and the addition of a press box and a new video-board.

Prior to coming to Southside, Simpson took over as Head Coach at Alabama Christian Academy in Montgomery, Alabama. During his tenure there, Simpson took over a team that had been 4-18 and led them to their first home playoff game in over 20-years. For his efforts he was named Montgomery Advertisers All-Metro Coach of the Year as well as being voted 4A Region 2 Coach of the Year (2010).

About the Author

Simpson also served as the head track coach at ACA and led the girls' and boys' teams to multiple top 10 finishes in 4A.

Simpson began his coaching career at Madison Academy, in Huntsville, Alabama. He served as a junior high basketball and football coach, before working into a varsity coaching role in football. He graduated from Harding University in 2003. He is married to Jamey and has three children: Avery, Braden and Bennett. The couple was married in 2001 after meeting at Harding University.

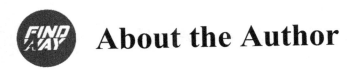

About the Author

Simpson's Books

Find A Way: What I Wish I'd Known When I Became A Head Football Coach

Coaching Football Like A Basketball Coach

Training Athletes Beyond The Game

Athletic Fundraising

Team Theme Book

Gun T System Books

Gun T Playbook

Gun T 2.0

Gun T Organizational Manual

Gun T Offensive Line Manual

Gun T Youth Manual

Defensive Books

34 Fit and Swarm Overview

Made in the USA
Monee, IL
30 July 2021

74385636R00066